# GRETCHEN WILSON

SPOTLIGHT PRESS L.L.C.

ISBN: 1-59670-107-2

Publishers: Peter L. Bannon and Joseph J. Bannon Sr.
Senior managing editor: Susan M. Moyer
Art director: K. Jeffrey Higgerson
Book design/Imaging: Heidi Norsen
Dust jacket design: Heidi Norsen
Project manager: Heidi Norsen
Photo editor: Erin Linden-Levy
Vice president of sales and marketing: Kevin King
Media and promotions managers: Nick Obradovich (regional),
        Randy Fouts (national), Maurey Williamson (print)

Printed in the United States

SP, L.L.C.
804 North Neil Street
Champaign, IL 61820

Phone: 1-877-424-2665
Fax: 217-363-2073

Front cover photo by CBS/Landov
Back cover photo by Frederick M. Brown/Getty Images

*"There's a LOT more 'Redneck Women' than 'High-Class Broads' out there! So just keep on keepin' on, Girlfriend!"*

*–Loretta Lynn*

# CONTENTS

*"It's great to see women empowered right now. People like Gretchen Wilson comin' along and makin' it easier for me to say NO to ever having to wear another dress."*

*–Terri Clark*

Tim McGraw, Gretchen Wilson, Lynyrd Skynyrd, Dickie Betts and Elvin Bishop joined forces for a **salute to Southern rock** at the 2005 Grammys in Los Angeles on February 13.

"Closing out the final concert of the 2005 CMA Music Festival on June 12, 2005 in Nashville, Tennessee, Wilson once again proved herself worthy of the commercial success and critical accolades that have come her way since the release of her debut single, "Redneck Woman," just 15 months ago. Now well past the potential danger of the introductory single casting her as a one-hit novelty act, Wilson seems well on her way to becoming one of the most important country artists to emerge during the past decade. Not that she's ever appeared timid in front of crowds, but Wilson's live perform-ances just keep getting better. She made her seven-song performance look virtually effortless during the show at the Coliseum, but that's a quality she shares with the finest performers of all musical genres."

–CMT

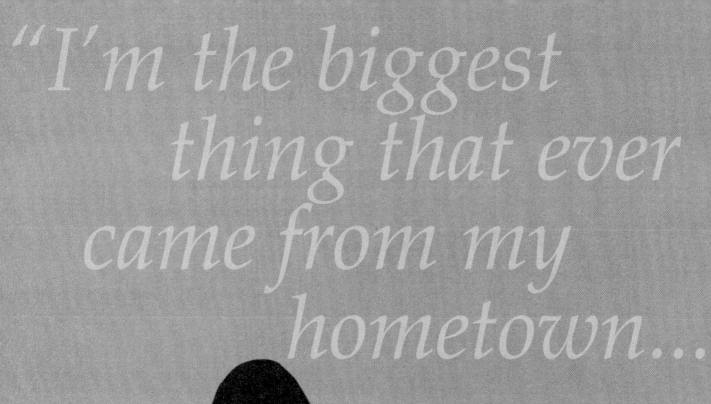

# "I'm the biggest thing that ever came from my hometown..."

## POCAHONTAS PROUD

**G**retchen Wilson was born on June 26, 1973, and grew up in the small Illinois town of Pocahontas, **population 727** (currently 850). Located 36 miles due east of St. Louis along Interstate 70, Pocahontas boasts a landscape of trailer parks and cornfields. Growing up in rural America wasn't easy for Gretchen or her family.

*"It's basic, but it's real. It's me."*
*—Gretchen on Pocahontas*

Gretchen's mother, Christine Heuer, was only 16 years old when Gretchen was born, and her father was no longer in the family picture from the time she was two. Gretchen grew up with folks who frequented the **Powhatan Restaurant,** located at the intersection of Pokey Road and I-70. Everyone knows everyone in Pocahontas and **there are no strangers**. Gretchen was right at home growing up in this small-town atmosphere.

AP/WWP

"To me it just seems so normal around there. It's my home. It's where I grew up. The faces around there look like my kind of people. I look at faces in other parts of the country and I don't get it right off the bat, but I look at anybody up there and it just looks like home."

–Gretchen on Pocahontas

**A PRETEEN PHOTOGRAPH OF GRETCHEN'S MOTHER, CHRISTINE HEUER.**

*"My mom made a lot of mistakes, but she was young. There were times we only had a little bit and times we didn't have anything, but she always made sure that we had love."*

–Gretchen on her mother

While her mother tried hard to provide for Gretchen and her younger brother Josh, the going was **not always easy**. Still, Gretchen always felt loved.

She was also lucky to have the **love and guidance** of her late grandparents, Vernon and Frances Heuer. "My grandma was the mainstay," says Gretchen. "She was the rock." Vernon, an army veteran, was a disagreeable old man who had lost a leg in World War II. A child of the Depression Era, Vernon stashed his money in a mason jar that he kept buried in the backyard.

*"When everything was going crazy and falling apart and we were moving around, my grandma had her head on straight. She lived a rough life and really never had anything, but she always had love for everybody."*

*–Gretchen on her grandmother's influence*

AP/WWP

Big O's, a bar five miles outside of town, provided an early informal education for Gretchen. It was owned by Mark Obermark, "Big O," a lifelong friend of Gretchen and her family. Dropping out of school after completing the eighth grade, Gretchen cooked and tended bar alongside her mom at the age of 14.

"Gretchen worked in the kitchen with her brother Josh and her mom tended bar," Obermark recalls, "but it was a small town, and a small place, so when things would get busy, Gretchen would jump behind the bar to serve drinks. Everybody worked hard and helped out."

*"I started singing about the same time I started walking and talking."*

–Gretchen on her music roots

## "At fifteen I was tending Big O's bar..."

MARK "BIG O" OBERMARK

"It was no big deal for her to be running the bar as a teenager," according to Big O. Reports that Gretchen had a loaded 12-gauge shotgun behind the bar just in case she needed a little extra persuasion or protection are exaggerated, Big O says. "There was a pistol under the cash register, and I always carried a pistol, but there were no shotguns. There were young kids in there drinking and there were school rivalries, so there was always something going on, and sometimes it got rough, but it wasn't too dangerous."

In Gretchen's early years, her home-town upbringing in Big O's along with her musical influences, including Tanya Tucker, Loretta Lynn and Patsy Cline, began to solidify her appreciation for and love of country music and its roots, which are often mired in misery.

"I could go back home to Big O's and jump behind the bar and just stay there all night with everybody, and I'd feel right at home."

–Gretchen Wilson

"I could feel the pain and I could only imagine what it was like to have an abusive husband and all the different things that she sang about."

–Gretchen on early musical influence Patsy Cline

*"Gretchen was always singing, always. She'd carry around a little recorder and sing in the bar. Then later she performed on a stage in my bar and others. She was always a great performer."*

*–"Big O"*

## Gretchen Wilson Park

LAND DONATED BY :

## American Legion Post 1104

___RULES___

OPEN DAYLIGHT TO 10:00pm....EXCEPT WITH PERMIT

PARK FACILITIES, FIRST COME BASIS...NO VEHICLES ON GRASS

NO BOAT MOTORS, EXCEPT ELECTRIC TROLLING MOTORS

HAND LINE FISHING ONLY 2 POLES PER PERSON LIMIT, NO GLASS BOTTLES

KEEP YOUR PARK CLEAN....VIOLATORS WILL BE PROSECUTED

PAR
OPP
DAYLI
UN
10

GRETCHEN CELEBRATING
A TEEN BIRTHDAY AT BIG O'S.

Gretchen met her father for the first time when she was 12 years old and learned that he played the guitar a little and sang some. She was told that he was once part of a band along with other members of his family. Even without formal music education, it was clear from a young age that Gretchen could sing.

She honed her craft in front of live audiences on stage at Big O's in an early version of karaoke; accompanied by popular country CDs, Gretchen would sing for tips .

She left home at 15 to sing in taverns and honky-tonks—her first paid gig was at the Hickory Daiquiri Dock Bar & Grill in Collinsville, Illinois.

*"Each man creates his own destiny. It's up to you what you're going to do with your life. It's not up to anybody else."*

*–Gretchen Wilson*

Eventually Gretchen took her country dreams to the next level and became a singer for a cover band, Baywolf, and started to really believe in her future in country music on a larger stage. Gretchen knew that it was up to her to create her own luck and chart her course for Nashville.

*"I was playing to Happy Hour crowds, an older generation of people. They thought I was adorable, and they liked hearing me, a 15-year-old, sitting there singing, 'You ain't woman enough to take my man.'"*

*–Gretchen Wilson*

*"It became apparent to me really fast that I wasn't going to be able to make a living and pay my bills playing on Broadway."*

*–Gretchen Wilson on her move to Nashville*

*"Spent my youth... singing truth, paying dues..."*

Gretchen arrived in Nashville in 1996 to pursue her dream of becoming a recording star. In the four years it took her to begin to live her dream, she returned to a job she was familiar with: serving drinks to customers on Printers Alley at the Bourbon Street Blues & Boogie Bar. Gretchen was willing to pay her dues and wasn't afraid to get her hands dirty while waiting for her future to become a reality.

## Gretchen's Musical Influences:
Loretta Lynn, Tanya Tucker, Ann Wilson, Patsy Cline

*"I knocked on every door on Music Row..."*

FRANK MICELOTTA/GETTY IMAGES

*"It's really just about being proud of who you are."*

Gretchen's future took a turn for the better one Friday night when Big Kenny Alphin and John Rich wandered into the bar where she was working for a couple of drinks. Gretchen was on stage singing a few songs, and John Rich was very impressed by her strong and original voice. When he asked Gretchen afterward why she didn't have a recording deal yet, she didn't take him seriously but gave him a demo she had made anyway. Then she went back to her real job.

"I guess I knew I could sing early on. Everybody told me I could, and they always had a good time listening, so I thought, 'Hey, you know, I could do this.' So it's been hard, I mean, it's chasing after a dream. But sometimes dreams come true."

–Gretchen Wilson

BIG KENNY ALPHIN AND JOHN RICH

AP/WWP

*"Her voice was just unbelievable. Just tear your face off."*

*–John Rich on hearing Gretchen sing for the first time*

*"I had so many unsuccessful showcases, and I was never really being given a good reason why they didn't want me. A lot of people in Nashville are looking for age, or beauty, or hair. I know people who, after one song, were told they were 'too country.' Too country? How could you be too country? It's country music! I wanted to make a record that sounded like the old stuff."*

*—Gretchen Wilson on her long road to fame*

### Gretchen's Desert Island Albums:
Patsy Cline's *Greatest Hits*, AC/DC's *Back In Black* and *The Essential Charlie Daniels*

John Rich attempted to contact Gretchen for months but she was busy by that time raising her daughter Gracy (Grace Frances Penner) and working hard to make ends meet. Finally, after much prodding by friends, Gretchen got back in touch with John Rich and he introduced her to a group of his friends who were also trying to make it on the Nashville country music scene.

Gretchen learned a lot about the behind-the-scenes innerworkings of Nashville music, songwriting and networking from John Rich. He also recruited her to become a member of the Muzik Mafia (Musically Artistic Friends In Alliance), a friendly and supportive collection of singers, songwriters and musicians and artists who encourage one another in their musical pursuits and play together at Nashville nightspots. In this warm but challenging atmosphere, Gretchen honed her songwriting skills and stage performance. Gretchen has written or co-written over 80 songs, some of which are collaborations with John Rich.

*"She had been turned down eight times for record deals by people who said that she wasn't pretty enough or that she was a 'Harley chick.'"*

—*John Rich*

KEVIN WINTER/GETTY IMAGES

"Gretchen Wilson is exactly what country music has needed desperately for a long time—a woman who is earthy, raucous, passionate, and extremely talented. You have to look to Tanya, Loretta and Dolly to find someone this real, this country, and this good."

—Rob Simbeck, "American Country Countdown"

AP/WWP

FRANK MICELOTTA/GETTY IMAGES

"We have almost that kind of brother-sister relationship. When we sit down to write a song, it almost takes on a life of its own. I guess he just knows me so well that it's almost like I'm writing with myself. He knows who I am and what I want to say."

—Gretchen Wilson on working with John Rich

AP/WWP

GRETCHEN DOESN'T LIKE IT WHEN PEOPLE REFER TO HER AS A SINGLE MOTHER. SHE AND HER BOYFRIEND, MIKE PENNER, HAVE RAISED GRACE TOGETHER SINCE HER BIRTH.

# "Holding you holds me together..."

In early 2004, Gretchen, her boyfriend, Mike Penner, and their daughter Grace lived in a small rented house in Mt. Juliet, surviving on Wilson's work as a demo singer. She would sing songs newly written by Nashville's top songwriters, recordings that were then pitched to major recording artists around town. The job brought anywhere from $200 to $1,200 a week, and sometimes she wouldn't get paid for sessions for at least six months.

Wilson would head to studios in the mornings, work all day and be home by 6 p.m. or so and have dinner that her boyfriend had made. After spending time with Mike and Grace, Wilson would stay up until 2 a.m. or later learning songs for the next day's sessions.

*"All the songs are excellent, my favorite being 'Pocahontas Proud' . . . that's a GREAT song and Ms. Wilson doesn't give a damn, she's singing from her heart. YOU GO GIRL."*

*–Internet fan quote*

AP/WWP

Everything changed when Gretchen signed a **recording contract** with Sony Music Nashville's Epic label. Fortunately for Gretchen and all of the fans who would come to appreciate her honesty and **down-to-earth** demeanor, Sony and its executives wanted Gretchen to just be herself and did not attempt to "spin" her image.

*"Halfway through my performance, I saw John begin writing on a piece of stationery. I watched him write an 'N' and then an 'O.' My heart sank, but I just tuned it out and finished the rest of the set. As we were leaving, John stopped me and said, 'I was going to slip this note to [another Sony executive] during your perform- ance, but I think you should have it instead.' I opened the note and read, 'NOW!' I have it framed and hanging on my wall."*

*–Gretchen on auditioning for Sony Music Nashville's John Grady*

AP/WWP

28

Gretchen has never been "the Barbie Doll type" and has no aspirations to become one of the **plastic beauty queens** who have pervaded "pop" country in recent years. Her refreshing take on having fun, kicking back and celebrating her **small-town roots** has won her a new legion of fans who were ready for a breath of fresh air on the country charts. With Gretchen, what you see is what you get.

> *"Move over, Loretta. Make way, Tanya. Here's another good ol' honky-tonk girl."*
>
> *–Internet fan quote*

AP/WWP

*"It would be hard for me to be more excited about a new artist than I am about Gretchen Wilson. The industry known as country music needs her desperately. Thank God she's signed with us."*

*–John Grady, Sony Music Nashville*

*"I may not be a ten but the boys say I clean up good..."*

"Gretchen was the best thing to happen to country music in 2004! Once you hear one of her hit songs on the radio you have a flavor for the album. She's got a great voice, full of feeling and passion. She uses her life experiences as a basis for her songs on this first album and her love of music shows through. If you're a fan of the classic country songs that tell a story, hers do...and she belts them out with gusto. Go Gretchen!"

—Internet fan quote

Of course, in addition to her obvious **vocal skills** and songwriting ability, Gretchen possesses some head-turning **physical attributes** that haven't exactly hurt her billboard aspirations, either. Her long, dark hair, her cool **"what are you lookin' at?" stare**, and athletic body in those skimpy spaghetti-strap tanks have made many a country convert. She fancies **tight jeans and belts** with large, metallic buckles. Gretchen is truly the whole package: undeniable talent combined with movie star sex appeal and media savvy.

*"I wanted to give a little high-five to the women from small town America. The women I grew up around are strong and proud of who they are. This is for them."*

*—Gretchen Wilson on "Redneck Woman"*

*"I just wanted to let you know my daughter who is only three years old loves your song 'Redneck Woman' and refers to it by 'The Hell Yeah' song. She knows the whole song word by word. She even had to get her own big guitar just like Gretchen, she says. We have to put your cd on every time we get in the car."*

**—Internet fan quote**

This rare combination of beauty and skill quickly catapulted Gretchen to the top of the charts in early 2004 when her first single, "Redneck Woman," hit the charts. An instant hit, "Redneck Woman" shot to number one on the Billboard country charts faster than any other country debut song since Billy Ray Cyrus went to the top slot with "Achy Breaky Heart" in 1992. It was also the first single by a solo female singer to top the Billboard country singles chart in over two years.

*"When she exploded, when she rose to the top, we had to do that, too. We just had to rise to the occasion, or we would be gone."*

*—Lisa D'Addario, Wilson's personal assistant and tour manager*

REUTERS/LANDOV

After the **incredible success** of her debut single, Gretchen spent time in the studio quickly completing her first album, *Here for the Party*, with producers Mark Wright and Joe Scaife and associate producer John Rich. Suddenly there was **great demand** for more Gretchen music as the country sought out Nashville's new phenomenon. The album was released **ahead of schedule** on May 11, 2004, due to the intense hype, and was so hot that it debuted at No. 1 on Billboard's country charts.

It also hit the pop album chart at **number two** with sales of 227,000 copies, the biggest opening week for a new country artist on record. Gretchen's throwback style, at a time when a lot of country music was leaning toward pop, was **immediately praised** as a long-awaited return to country's roots.

*"Definitely 'When I Think About Cheatin.' It reminds me of something that could have been recorded 30 years ago. Patsy Cline could have had a hit with this song. I love the chord progressions and the steel guitar. And I'm really proud of being a writer on it. Through the years, there have been so many songs written about cheating, but this song has a different twist. It's a cheating song with a happy ending."*

*—Gretchen Wilson on her favorite song on her debut album*

REUTERS/LANDOV

*"I think we needed a new female singer who wasn't a cookie cutter. I think she has guts and spunk and she's cute as hell! And to think no one wanted to sign her...bet those record execs are kicking themselves right now! She is in a class of very few!"*

**—Internet fan quote**

*"I've had my share of fights. I always tell people to be careful, because if you see my earrings come out, you know I'm getting ready to go."*

*—Gretchen Wilson*

"When you grow up singing in bar bands you can't imagine people having conference calls from New York to L.A. to Nashville all
about you. It helps an artist to really trust her management. Even
a seasoned artist can make some big mistakes."

–Gretchen Wilson on coping with the demands of fame

The release of *Here for the Party* in 2004 started a wild ride for Gretchen. Her life was turned upside down with numerous media appearances and performances on award shows and in concert, where in the summer of 2004, she toured with Brooks & Dunn and Montgomery Gentry, and later in 2005 with Kenny Chesney.

EPA/LANDOV

*"The honesty of this album hits you squarely between the eyes from the first song. This is not your daddy's old country music —no sirree. Forget the old moon, spoon and June routines, forget cryin' and leavin' and broken hearts, this is solar plexus-bustin' rocking country from a new burst of fresh air on the country scene."*

**–Internet fan quote**

*"It is a relief to no longer live paycheck to paycheck. I think the main thing that's changed, I feel like a big burden of big worry has been lifted."*

*–Gretchen Wilson*

FRANK MICELOTTA/GETTY IMAGES

Gretchen's life has certainly changed a lot in 2004 and 2005. While she has been hailed as an **overnight success**, those close to her story know that it was a lifetime in the making. She is still getting used to the acclaim and sudden financial security that her fame has brought her.

*"What in the world has Gretchen Wilson done?! What no other female country artist has been able to do in years, she has brought back a style and sound that has been missing or reserved for the men for far too long. That strong outlaw country woman that can hold her own with the men and isn't afraid to let that attitude show. In an industry where there are entirely too many "carbon copy" artists Gretchen stands alone. This is the album to buy for a new old country music that is long overdue,thanks Gretchen!!"*

*–Internet fan quote*

While the whirlwind Gretchen has found herself in has certainly been life changing, she **stays grounded** by making time at home with her daughter, running the vacuum and doing laundry. It's more difficult these days to shop at Wal-Mart or go to the grocery, but Gretchen tries to keep life **as normal as possible** for her daughter and those around her. When she can't be at home, she travels with her daughter, Grace, boyfriend Mike Penner, and other family members.

AP/WWP

**GRETCHEN WITH BOYFRIEND MIKE PENNER.**

*"It was crazy. I don't think anybody can really prepare you for what happens. Nobody can educate you on the road, so you just get out there and do it. I'm still in the beginning stages. I think it's awesome when I get recognized and then the autographs and the meet and greets are just incredible. That's right behind performing. But yeah, it's a lot to handle in a short amount of time."*

*–Gretchen Wilson on adjusting to fame*

*"I'm just a simple, ordinary woman. And I think that what I'm trying to say is that it's really cool to be that. I think that's why people have really connected with me; I'm just like them."*

—Gretchen Wilson

"She hasn't changed at all. I see her becoming more sophisticated because she has to deal with so many things now, but she was always really smart."

–Tour manager Mike Oswald

"I've got to tell you something
else: You have to work for it.
Dreams don't just happen.
You have to work for it, and you
have to take the good with the
bad. In the case of what
I'm doing, you have to change
your life."

—Gretchen Wilson on
achieving dreams

"I guess the most memorable thing so far was about a month after my single was released I took a surprise trip back home to a small bar where all this started for me. I tried to show up unannounced, but word got out, and there were a lot of people there. I played 'Pocahontas Proud' for the first time in Pocahontas before the record even came out. The reaction of the crowd there was just overwhelming. There was just thunderous applause, people were laughing, people were crying, some were screaming . . . it was just amazing."

–Gretchen on memorable moments of the past year

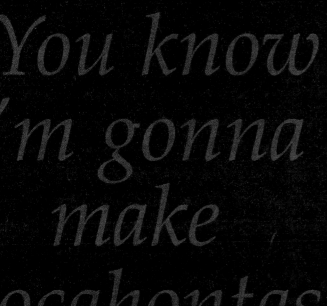

*"Be honest and just be proud of yourself. Always, always be true to yourself. It's a tough business and a lot of people have a lot of different ideas, and things they think an artist needs to be, in order to be successful. If you know you've got something, don't let the world tweak what you've got. Your fans know what's real."*

*–Gretchen Wilson's advice to newcomers*

AP/WWP

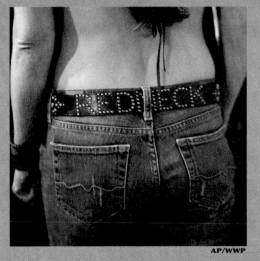
AP/WWP

*"I heard a brief snippet of 'Homewrecker' which made me laugh out loud. I am not a real fan of contemporary country music, actually most of it makes we want to stick pencils in my eyes. But while Gretchen Wilson has more than her share of attitude and moxie, she also has an amazingly soulful voice that grabs you and takes you along on her more tender and heartfelt songs."*

*–Internet fan quote*

Gretchen is looking forward to being part of a **new record label** that is being built by the Muzik Mafia and she eventually **hopes to mentor** other up-and-coming musicians the way John Rich mentored her.

What a year 2004 was for Gretchen Wilson! A platinum album many times over, sell-out concert venues, awards every time she turned around. And on December 19, **Ed Bradley interviewed Gretchen** on the popular CBS show *60 Minutes*.

This top-rated news show followed Gretchen to **Pocahontas and to Nashville** and documented her rise to fame. Ed Bradley talked frankly with Gretchen about her small-town upbringing, her struggles on the road to success and how life changed for her after her record deal.

Together Wilson and Bradley visited **historical Ryman Auditorium** in Nashville, where Gretchen snuck in with John Rich before she was "discovered," and sang, "If You've Got Leavin' On Your Mind." They also visited Tootsies Orchid Lounge in Nashville and toured "both sides of the tracks" in Gretchen's hometown of Pocahontas, Illinois.

Gretchen shared with Bradley and the viewing audience her opinion that being a redneck is "knowing how to **live with what you have**, not worrying about what you don't have."

*"You try to take that dream as far as it will get you. I want to do it all. I've only begun to scratch the surface of what I can accomplish in this industry."*

*–Gretchen Wilson on the future*

**Gretchen Wilson** won the Break-through Artist Award (in all genres) at the 2004 **American Music Awards.** Gretchen also provided one of the evening's best live performances with her sassy debut smash, "Redneck Woman." Gretchen joined Christina Aguilera, Lauryn Hill, Avril Lavigne, Britney Spears, Alanis Morissette and six other talented women whose debut albums hit the **three-million mark** within six months of their release dates.

# MUSICALLY ARTISTIC

*"Life's as large as you want to make it."*

*–John Rich*

Big Kenny Alphin, a rock 'n' roll singer, and John Rich, a country singer, gathered with their friends to play music at the tiny Pub of Luv in Nashville starting in October of 2001, while hoping to secure a recording contract.

They formed a loose-knit group that called itself the Muzik Mafia (Musically Artistic Friends In Alliance), and their sessions grew to include a painter, juggler, fire eater, dancing dwarf, rapping cowboy and an unknown singer named Gretchen Wilson. "The Godfathers" of the Mafia include Cory Gierman, Big Kenny Alphin, John Rich, and Jon Nicholson. The Godfathers' main mission was to share a love of music with whomever walked in the door with no prejudices.

*"Go cowboy Go cowboy Go..."*

FRIENDS IN ALLIANCE

54

# "Music without Prejudice..."

As their popularity spread, the crowds responded to their unique brand of music, and Big & Rich and Gretchen Wilson went on to sell more than five million albums between them. They made a large contribution to the 12 percent increase in 2004 in country music sales. Those in the industry who weren't familiar with the Muzik Mafia are paying more attention now after their success at this year's Grammys. The Muzik Mafia has been compared to artists like Waylon Jennings, Merle Haggard Jr., and Willie Nelson and their experimentation with country music in the 1970s.

*"Hi, Big & Rich, I just wanted to let you know that I sincerely love what you are doing in the music industry. I also admire the way you are promoting love for everyone. I am in a wheelchair and prejudice is something that I have had to deal with quite often in my 29 years on this earth. If there were more people like you in this world, it would be a much better place to be. Lots of luck in all you do!"*

*—Internet fan quote*

*"To my musical brothers, I have been following your application of commitment, and I must say I have been deeply moved and inspired. Your conception of the MAFIA has restored some of my long-lost faith in 'strength in numbers' approach to this business we call music. Please keep kickin' those doors open, there's a lot of us left out here still searchin' for the entrance."*

*–Internet fan quote*

*"It was a celebration. We never took money out of it, never charged anybody to come, and anybody who had some kind of performance, we'd let 'em get up there."*

*–Big Kenny Alphin*

# "Just wanna hear everybody sing..."

GRETCHEN WILSON 57

RUSTY RUSSELL/GETTY IMAGES

## WHAT THEY'RE SAYING ABOUT BIG & RICH AND THE MUZIK MAFIA. . .

" . . . a renegade group of Music City misfits."

**"funny and irreverent"**

"It ain't your parents country music."

"Big & Rich are exactly what country music needed. They truly are a breath of fresh air in a genre of music that is becoming...well, bland."

**"very raw energy"**

"They will make you laugh, cry and sing at the top of your lungs."

# 'Horse of a Different Color' is just plain FUN."

"It is so refreshing to hear music that runs the gamut from provocative and crazy to serious issues such as domestic abuse. . . . "

"They bring something for everybody."

"*. . . the perfect example of Country gone Rock, flirting with Hip-Hop. . . .*"

# *"Love Everybody!"*

"They prove you don't have to feed into musical sterotypes."

Great Music, Great Mood, Great Writing!"

"a magnificent blend of country with a little bit of rap and a lot of amazing harmonies. . . . "

AP/WWP

"There was a void for that style of music. I think the time was right for the Muzik Mafia to hit. There was no artist around at the time like Gretchen Wilson, and Big & Rich brought an innovative style."

—Jeff Walker, owner of Aristo Media

*"It feels like we haven't seen a breath of fresh air like this in maybe 10 years. They are outspoken and seem to be incredible freethinkers who don't let boundaries get in the way of the music they want to play."*

*–Paul Villadolid, vice president of programming and development for CMT*

"*I'm the only John Wayne left in this town...*"

Country Music Television (CMT) ran a six-part weekly series on the group, called "Muzik Mafia TV." It showed the members of the Mafia on tour, gave in-depth portrayals of the members, and included live performances.

*"We are here for one reason. ...To share our love of music..."*

John Rich: *"You know what you are, Big Kenny?"*

Big Kenny: *"What?"*

John Rich: *"You're a planet."*

Big Kenny: *"Well, you're a planet, too."*

John Rich: *"You know what happens when two planets collide?"*

Big Kenny: *"What?"*

John Rich: *"You get a whole new universe."*

Big & Rich's debut album, *Horse Of A Different Color*, mixed country with rap and rock; their first single was a catchy tune with sexual overtones called "Save A Horse, Ride A Cowboy." All of the Mafia members were in the video, including Gretchen Wilson, who drove a tractor. They followed up that smash debut with hits "Holy Water" and "Big Time."

AP/WWP

"*What so impressed me in my first meeting with Kenny and John is that these are not just two redneck guys out on just any kind of a mission. They may play their music loud and stir up a crowd into a party frenzy, but they have a real message to tell as well. This message, like their movement, is a simple one: LOVE EVERYBODY!*"

*–Christine Bohorfoush, AngryCountry.com staff writer*

FRANK MICELOTTA/FOX/GETTY IMAGES

*"I don't think that it's just really rap. I think it's just that people are starting to learn from each other. I think that by combining different styles of music, everybody gets a chance to learn from each other and gets to interpret different things into their musical style, and it makes them grow in their own genre."*

*–Gretchen Wilson on the combination of rap and country audiences*

# Muzik Mafia

## The Godfathers:

Cory Gierman, Big Kenny, John Rich, and Jon Nicholson

## Mafia Members:

**Gretchen Wilson,** singer/songwriter, guitar player

**Jon Nicholson,** singer/songwriter, keyboard player

**James Otto,** singer/songwriter, guitar player

**Cowboy Troy, aka Troy Coleman,** 6'5" black rapping cowboy

**Dean Hall,** singer/songwriter/athlete, newest Mafia member

**Shannon Lawson,** guitar player of bluegrass/rock n roll

**Chance, aka Timothy C Smith,** Southern hip-hop country rapper/singer

**Mista D,** musician with a goal to "change the atmosphere" through music

**Rachel Kice,** a "painter of fine music", she captures the mafia on stage

**Two-foot Fred, aka "The Deuce",** Freddie Gill performs with the Mafia

JOHN STANTON/GETTY IMAGES

## The Mafia Pit:

On any given night supporting musicians (Pitbosses) might include:

Max on the sax

Pino Squillace

Brian Barnett

The Reverend Elijah DD Holt on percussion

Jerry Navarro on the bass

Adam Shoenfeld on guitar

"We all said that whoever gets up there will help pull the others up. Her success helped us, and our success helped her."

–Big Kenny Alphin

*"I want my music to represent what I do live, which it is really bluegrass rock 'n' roll. People seem to love it, because it's earthy and simple and it rocks."*

*—Shannon Lawson, Mafia member*

AP/WWP

Mafia member Shannon Lawson combines his bluegrass origins and rural Kentucky roots to create music that reflects his background in R&B, funk and rock bands. His dynamic voice, guitar playing and raw energy offer a unique sound that is all Shannon.

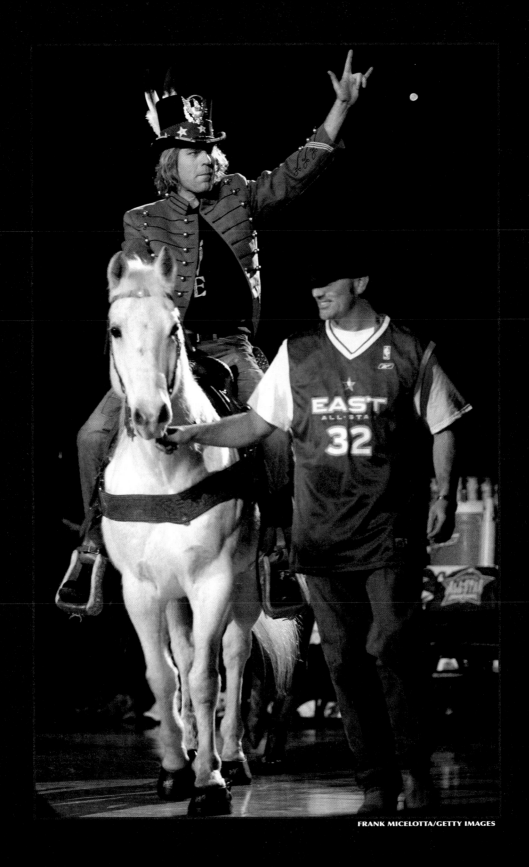

*"I learn something new about myself every time I deal with Muzik Mafia."*

*–Gretchen Wilson*

Mafia member Troy Coleman, aka Cowboy Troy, was featured in a *USA Today* article in March of 2005. He is the latest of the Muzik Mafia members to emerge, following in the footsteps of Big & Rich and Gretchen Wilson. Born in Victoria, Texas, Cowboy Troy toured with Big & Rich and Tim McGraw in 2004 and his current single, "I Play Chicken With the Train," was the first hit off of his debut album, *Loco Motive*. Troy grew up listening to country, rock music, and rap, leading to the development of his self-described style of music—"hick-hop." In the liner notes to his debut album he lists his heroes, starting with Charlie Daniels and Jerry Reed. Even now, he quickly cites Daniels and Reed (as well as Dwight Yoakam) as the country artists he'd most like to work with. "If they're out there listening, please tune in. Please call!" he says, enthusiastically.

**FRANK MICELOTTA/GETTY IMAGES**

*"My main concern as an artist and as a songwriter is to make sure I not only write good songs but also perform them well. I don't get so much bent out of shape if someone has an opinion, because people are entitled to their opinion. I can respect the fact that they can voice their opinions as they choose."*

—*Cowboy Troy*

*"Sometimes they feel like somebody's slammed a lightning bolt upside their head. Which we like to do every now and then. I mean, it's fun to shake stuff up by bringing out your Mandarin Chinese-rapping black cowboy godfather."*

*–John Rich*

*"If it moves my soul I'm gonna keep rollin', rollin'..."*

Gretchen Wilson was the Mafia's first breakout artist after "Redneck Woman" hit the charts. Gretchen gives kudos to the Muzik Mafia, whom she says supported her during her climb to the top.

Big & Rich and Gretchen Wilson are no longer able to participate in weekly shows with the Mafia due to their own schedules, but the core group is still going strong. Many of the Mafia soldiers still interact and perform together, offering one another support and encouragment along the rocky road to fame.

*"We just wanted a place we could play and not have to clean up afterward."*

*–Big Kenny Alphin*

# GRETCHEN'S LUCKY NUMBER

# 27

You've seen Gretchen with the number 27 several times. For her pre-show Super Bowl performance, she came on the field with a jersey number of her own: 27.

Those close to the redneck woman know they have arrived in her inner circle when she presents them with a dog tag with the number 27 on it.

So why 27?

Gretchen was 27 when she had her daughter, Grace; the first week's sales of her first album, *Here for the Party,* numbered 227,000; the official population of her hometown of Pocahontas in 2000 was 727 and she has since adopted it as a number that has brought her luck in her life.

"It's kind of an insider laminate."
*–Gretchen Wilson on the lucky No. 27 dog tags*

Gretchen started wearing a No. 27 dog tag and gave them to select people in her band, on her management team, at her record label, and in the Muzik Mafia.

Those who are lucky enough to receive a No. 27 dog tag from Gretchen understand and treasure its importance, especially singers in the Muzik Mafia. James Otto cried when he got his.

Kid Rock, Hank Williams, Jr., Tanya Tucker and Big & Rich all make guest appearances in Gretchen's first video, "Redneck Woman." Gretchen met Kid Rock in Nashville at a Muzik Mafia event. The two got along well and Kid asked Gretchen to come to his Chattanooga concert where she joined him onstage to sing his hit song "Picture."

> ## *"I've got posters on my wall of Skynard, KID and Strait"*

*"I'd have to say it would be the trailer scene with Bobby [Kid Rock] and Hank [Williams Jr.]. They were a lot of fun."*

*—Gretchen Wilson on what she remembers most about making the "Redneck Woman" video*

*"Are you kidding me? I've had a baby."*

— Gretchen Wilson, on whether her
first tattoo (the No. 27) hurt

In early 2005, Gretchen and six people in her posse showed up at Tattoo Mania on Sunset Strip in Los Angeles and got "27" tattooed on their right ankles, a place some people say can be painful for getting tattooed.

REUTERS/LANDOV

"Good music is good music. . . . I grew up listening to Tanya and Hank and Merle and all that kind of stuff. But at the same time, I was listening to Skynyrd and AC/DC. . . . Today, if you were to look at my CD collection, it might scare some people. . . . I think music can heal your soul if you'll let it. I think everybody should like all different kinds of music. I don't think anybody should be stuck to just one thing. It should be what you like, not what it's classified as."

—Gretchen Wilson on playing and
appreciating different styles of music

# SHE'S A REDBIRD WOMAN

*"I grew up in Pocahontas, Illinois, about 35 miles east of St. Louis. Some of my best childhood memories are of family, friends and the Cardinals on TV. When this opportunity came up, it just seemed natural for me to sing a song for my team. Thanks Cards, for the memories!"*

*–Gretchen Wilson on "I've Got Redbird Fever"*

RICH PILLING/MLB PHOTOS/GETTY IMAGES

In the fall of 2004, Gretchen Wilson and NBC affiliate KSDK, NewsChannel 5 teamed up to write the song, "I've Got Redbird Fever" to the tune of the No. 1 hit "Redneck Woman," to honor her beloved St. Louis Cardinals.

The song was featured on promotional spots on NewsChannel 5, and was used in programming content during sports coverage of the World Series.

"*Let me get a big*

*'Go Cards' from*

"*I hope this song helps rally not only country music fans, but everyone who is a part of the Cardinal nation.*"

–Gretchen Wilson

*you Redbird*

*fans tonight,*

*'GO CARDS!'*"

# GRETCHEN'S DEBUT IN THE THE COUNTRY SPOTLIGHT

KEVIN WINTER/GETTY IMAGES

## 2004

**March:** Sony Music Nashville released Gretchen's first single, "Redneck Woman."

**May 11:** *Here for the Party* debuts.

**May 26:** (photo at left) Gretchen performed "Redneck Woman" at the Academy of Country Music awards show on CBS. It was her first prime-time major network performance.

OPPOSITE PAGE: GRETCHEN WILSON POSES FOR A PORTRAIT DURING THE 2004 BILLBOARD MUSIC AWARDS AT THE MGM GRAND GARDEN ARENA ON DECEMBER 8, 2004 IN LAS VEGAS, NEVADA.

FRANK MICELOTTA/GETTY IMAGES

GRETCHEN WILSON

*"Dang it, whoever said that Gretchen wasn't pretty enough? What, because she isn't blonde-haired and blue-eyed? Or the perfect type of ingenue that hollywood looks for? Country music was never ruled by Hollywood. It is all about the music and the heart."*

*—Internet fan quote*

**June:** *Here for the Party* topped the Billboard country chart—the first time a new artist debuted at No. 1 on the chart.

"Redneck Woman" topped the Billboard country singles chart.

*Here for the Party* was certified platinum.

**June 2:** Wilson sang "Redneck Woman" on NBC's *Today* show and she was interviewed by Matt Lauer. During her first trip to New York City she visited the famous Hogs & Heifers Saloon. Her beige Target bra was added to the celebrity underwear collection behind the bar.

**June 13:** (photo on opposite page) Gretchen perfomed at the 2004 CMA Music Festival. The four-day event, held annually in Nashville, Tennessee, is the largest festival in country music.

**June 18:** Gretchen performed "Here for the Party" on NBC's *Tonight Show*.

**July:** *Here for the Party* was certified double platinum.

WENN/LANDOV

**October 25:** (photo above) Gretchen and Muzik Mafia buddies Big & Rich performed a medley for NBC's Radio Music Awards. Ashlee Simpson attended as well, still recovering from her lip-synching debacle on *Saturday Night Live*. Gretchen sought Simpson out and offered support and the moment was later televised on Simpson's reality show.

**October 27:** A huge St. Louis Cardinals fan, Gretchen sang the national anthem in St. Louis before World Series Game 4 between the Cardinals and the Boston Red Sox. Baseball legend Lou Brock asked Gretchen for an autograph.

REUTERS/LANDOV

**November 9:** Wilson (photo on left) performed "When I Think About Cheatin'" on the Country Music Association awards show on CBS, where she won the Horizon award (photo on opposite page).

*"I came here last year and sat way back there in the back and dreamed of standing up here one day. I never dreamed it would happen this soon."*

*–Gretchen Wilson on winning the Horizon Award*

GRETCHEN WILSON ACCEPTS HER HORIZON AWARD AT THE 38TH ANNUAL CMA AWARDS AT THE GRAND OLE OPRY HOUSE NOVEMBER 9, 2004, IN NASHVILLE, TENNESSEE.

*"I knew when I started singing at 15 what I wanted to do with my life. What did I need high school for? How was it gonna help me? But I wish I had finished high school. My mom never finished high school, either. My mom and I are thinking about getting our GEDs together."*

*–Gretchen Wilson on dropping out of school*

INTERNET FAN POSTS DESCRIBING
**GRETCHEN** IN A WORD OR SENTENCE:

"Humble"    "Right on Sista"    "Muddin' in a 4 x 4"

"That's a big HELL YEAH"    "Real"    "That's our girl"

"Homewreckers LOOK OUT, cause
she's gonna kick some butt. . ."

"A true down-home country girl"    "Heart of gold"

"Best female singer since
Patsy Cline"

"The Mafia Queen!!!"

"Great guitar player"    "She's a Wal-Mart shopper"

"A strong woman, hear her ROAR!"

"Wonderful mom"    "Pocahontas Proud"

"Wanna be like her when i grow up. . ."

"True to herself"

"Nothing's fake about her. . ."

"Go Gretchen Go!!! We love ya girl!!!"

FRANK MICELOTTA/GETTY IMAGES

Gretchen has been wowing sold-out crowds across the country touring with Kenny Chesney and Uncle Kracker. At a concert on March 26, 2005 in St. Paul, Minnesota, she surprised Chesney with a special rendition on his birthday. After Kenny introduced her, she took a bow, the band stopped, and then she suddenly burst into "Happy Birthday" in Marilyn Monroe style. "Happy birthday, Mr. Chesney," she sang, and then handed Kenny a huge tropical drink.

FRANK MICELOTTA/GETTY IMAGES

"*I hope the next outing from Ms. Wilson will be this much fun. If it is, we better block off a whole city section for this party...it's too hot to handle!*"

**–Internet fan quote**

**November:** *Here for the Party* was certified triple platinum.

**November 14:** Gretchen won the Break-through Artist award (photo above) on the American Music Awards show, where she also performed "Redneck Woman." She was also nominated for Favorite Female Country Artist.

REUTERS/LANDOV

**December:** *Here for the Party* was the fifth biggest-selling LP in the U.S. for the year, with sales topping 2.9 billion.

Gretchen topped the Billboard year-end charts as the top female country artist, top new country artist, and top female country album artist.

**December 7:** Wilson joined Kanye West, the Black-Eyed Peas and actor Kevin Spacey in Los Angeles to announce Grammy nominations (photo above).

**December 8:** Wilson (photo on opposite page) won best female country artist and best new country artist during the Billboard Music Awards. *American Idol* judge Paula Abdul interviewed Wilson backstage while *Idol* judge Randy Jackson proclaimed, "I love Gretchen Wilson."

**December 19:** CBS's *60 Minutes* featured Gretchen Wilson. Correspondent Ed Bradley drank bottled water while Wilson sucked down longneck beers during an interview at Tootsie's honky-tonk on Lower Broadway in Nashville. They also visited her hometown of Pocahontas.

*"Everybody would probably say 'Devil Went Down to Georgia,' but I think my favorite is probably 'In America.'"*

*–Gretchen on her favorite Charlie Daniels song*

JED JACOBSOHN/GETTY IMAGES

*"Gretchen's album is FUN! Yes, I said it...FUN! I think a lot of people like her because she likes to have a good time, and with the way the world is today, we need some music like that every now and then!"*

*–Internet fan quote*

# 2005

**February 6, 2005:** Gretchen performed "Here for the Party" in a pregame performance with one of her idols, Charlie Daniels, at Super Bowl XXXIX (photo above and on opposite page).

**February 13, 2005:** Gretchen won a Grammy award for best female country vocal performance and was nominated for best country song, "Redneck Woman" (awarded to the songwriter), Best country album for *Here for the Party* and best new artist. Gretchen performed at the ceremony.

**Late February, 2005:** Gretchen toured Australia, and is planning her new album with Mark Wright and John Rich of Big & Rich, who produced her debut. The album, *All Jacked Up*, will be released September 27, 2005.

*Here for the Party* is quadruple platinum.

*"Redneck women, look out!!! This cd is truly gnarly in every sense of the word. This rural gang-star comes out with witty country slang accompanied by those great banjo solos craved by the purest country music listeners. Definitely a must buy for anyone looking to feel like an urban cowboy/girl."*

*–Internet fan quote*

GRETCHEN WILSON ACCEPTS HER VIDEO AWARD AT THE CMT MUSIC AWARDS APRIL 11, 2005, IN NASHVILLE, TENNESSEE.

**April 11, 2005:** Wilson added to her status as country music's hottest newcomer after winning two awards at the 2005 CMT Music Awards (photo above). Wilson won Breakthrough Video of the Year for "Redneck Woman"and Female Video of the Year for "When I Think About Cheatin'."

**May 17, 2005:** Gretchen won Top Female Vocalist and Top New Artist at the Academy of Country Music awards. Gretchen was nominated for five awards, including top new artist, top female vocalist, video of the year for "Redneck Woman," single of the year for "Redneck Woman," and album of the year for *Here for the Party*.

RUSTY RUSSELL/GETTY IMAGES

GRETCHEN WILSON ACCEPTS THE BEST FEMALE VIDEO AWARD AT THE CMT MUSIC AWARDS APRIL 11, 2005, IN NASHVILLE, TENNESSEE.

*"I want to say thank you again to the fans for believing in me and for making this one of the most incredible years of my life. Thank you, Miss Reba McEntire for being an incredible inspiration to me, and also Martina McBride. I can't even believe I'm in the same category with these ladies, but thank you so much for this. It means the world to me."*

*—Gretchen Wilson on receiving best female video award at 2005 CMT Awards*

*"I'm an artist that has been extremely lucky. Things came very easy for me with 'Redneck Woman' being as big a hit as it was."*

—*Gretchen Wilson at the 2005 CMT Awards*

RUSTY RUSSELL/GETTY IMAGES

**GRETCHEN WILSON PERFORMS WITH ANN WILSON OF HEART AT THE CMT MUSIC AWARDS APRIL 11, 2005, IN NASHVILLE, TENNESSEE.**

LORETTA LYNN (CENTER) PREPARES TO ACCEPT THE VISIONARY AWARD AS MARTINA McBRIDE (LEFT) AND GRETCHEN WILSON (RIGHT) LOOK ON DURING THE CMT MUSIC AWARDS APRIL 11, 2005, IN NASHVILLE, TENNESSEE.

*"The day I seen Gretchen come out and do 'Redneck Woman,' I said, 'There's a smash. She's the next girl singer.'"*

*—Loretta Lynn on Gretchen Wilson at the 2005 CMT Awards*

GRETCHEN WILSON PERFORMS ONSTAGE AT THE SECOND ANNUAL NEW ARTIST SHOW AT THE MANDALAY BAY RESORT ON MAY 16, 2005, IN LAS VEGAS, NEVADA.

As a precursor to the May 17 Academy of Country Music Awards, the five nominees for the new artist prize, won by Gretchen Wilson, performed at a concert at the Mandalay Bay Resort & Casino. Gretchen opened with "All Jacked Up," the title track of her upcoming album. Wilson had the distinct advantage of opening plenty of shows in huge venues during Kenny Chesney's current tour. A natural entertainer, Gretchen has made the transition from clubs, and it's only a matter of time before she's headlining her own tour of arenas and amphitheaters.

At the new artist show, Wilson sang another new song, "Politically Uncorrect," which she'll sing with Merle Haggard on her new album. The other three songs she performed were immediately identifiable for everyone in the room: "Homewrecker," "Redneck Woman" and "Here for the Party."

"It's a lot to get used to. The hardest part for me is the time I have to spend away from my daughter. But I got to the point where I now have two buses rollin' and every once in a while she comes with me, and she loves the bus. When Grace is on it, the bus is more like Disneyland on wheels. We've got cartoons and toys all over the place. . . .we picked up a puppy in Samford, Florida, and that's her name, Samford. It's a cute little dog and she does real good on the bus and it's real good to have her around."

–Gretchen Wilson on the trials of touring

"I have never been much of a country fan, but Gretchen's music has now got me 100% now. I have my ring tone on my cell phone 'Redneck Woman.' I just cannot get enough of her music. She is really proud of her upbringing and has made women stand up and say, 'Hell Yeah!'"

–Internet fan quote

*"Being a redneck is just a way of life. It's where I came from. . . .
I don't think you have to live in a trailer park to be a redneck.
I don't think you have to drive a truck to be a redneck."*

–Gretchen Wilson

# GretcHen Hands out WHeels to Cancer Survivors

Gretchen Wilson teamed up with Chevrolet in January of 2005 to help distribute new vehicles to a lucky few. Ten young cancer survivors in the Nashville area received brand new 2005 Chevy Cobalts to help them ring in the new year.

During "America's Party with Ryan Seacrest" on New Year's Eve at the Opryland Hotel, Gretchen announced that the ten recipients, aged 19-30, would be driving home the new vehicles. The cars were donated by Chevrolet to the T.J. Martell Foundation, which raises funds for research and treatment of various forms of leukemia, other cancers and AIDS.

The T.J. Martel Foundation collaborated with the Vanderbilt-Ingram Cancer center in selecting the lucky recipients. With the help of many generous sponsors, volunteers and celebrities, the Martell Foundation hosts a variety of fundraising events throughout the year, including galas, auctions, wine dinners, walk-a-thons and golf tournaments. Over the last 28 years, the Martell Foundation has grown due to the hard work and generosity primarily of the music industry with additional support from individuals and companies focused on finding the cure.

# Country in the Rockies XI

Gretchen Wilson and Big & Rich were headliners for "Country in the Rockies XI", which is the premier celebrity ski event of the country music industry, held at Club Med Crested Butte, Colorado, in February of 2005.

This event gave guests opportunities to ski and socialize with the award-winning Muzik Mafia members and many other musical acts performed. Alpine skiing and snowboarding along with great music are the main attractions of the event, but there is also snowshoeing, cross-country skiing and horseback riding. Participants also enjoy all-star concerts and a celebrity-hosted happy hour in downtown Crested Butte along with auctions for travel, artwork, jewelry and celebrity memorabilia.

Country in the Rockies is the main fundraiser of the T.J. Martell Foundation's Nashville Division. Since 1993, the Martell Foundation has enabled physicians and scientists of the Frances Williams Preston Laboratories, a Vanderbilt-Ingram Cancer Center, to conduct and pioneer new findings to transfer from laboratories to patients. To date, the Nashville Division has raised $13 million in support of Vanderbilt-Ingram Cancer Center's projects. These contributions have paved the way for additional funding totaling more than $100 million from public and private sources to further advance ongoing efforts to alleviate suffering from cancer.

*"The mission: To change and save lives..."*

AP/WWP

GRETCHEN ARRIVES AT THE 2004 RADIO MUSIC AWARDS HELD AT THE ALADDIN RESORT AND CASINO IN LAS VEGAS, NEVADA, ON OCTOBER 25, 2004.

Hey Gretchen!
 My name is Kaitie Cooley and
I live in Paxton, IL. I absolutely
love your music. I think your music is
Cool, fun, sassy, and hip. Thats how I describe
your music. I listen to "I'm here for the
Party", "Redneck Woman", and "When I think
about Cheaten". I cant wait to go to a
concert of yours. Mabey I can meet
you some time. I also want to be a singer
too.
                    Your Best Fan, Kaitie Cooley (age 9)

Gretchen

anyone else who's out there that's hopeful, that doesn't fit the right mold, that doesn't weigh exactly a buck twenty, doesn't have the right color hair and all that stuff that a lot of people seem to think is what you've got to be and what you've got to have to make it . . . I hope that if I've done anything, I can make those girls out there see that just being yourself, being honest and being real is the most rewarding thing you can do. I can tell you flat-out that I would not want to be standing here holding these awards and talking to you if I hadn't been completely honest and been myself the whole way."

—Gretchen Wilson after winning the 2005 ACM Top Female

Dear Gretchen...
my favorite song is Redneck Woman.
I am in Kindergarten. Mom won't
let me say all the words.
Sophie

GRETCHEN WILSON PERFORMS ONSTAGE AT THE SECOND ANNUAL NEW ARTIST SHOW AT THE MANDALAY BAY RESORT ON MAY 16, 2005 IN LAS VEGAS, NEVADA.

Gretchen Wilson and Sony Music Nashville will release Gretchen's second album, *All Jacked Up*, on September 27, 2005. Wilson co-produced the album with Mark Wright and Big & Rich's John Rich, and she wrote or co-wrote seven of the 12 songs. Before going on tour with Kenny Chesney, Wilson spent the early part of the year recording the project, and has already been performing several songs on tour from the upcoming album, including the upbeat "All Jacked Up" title track, "Skoal Ring," "California Girls" and "Politically Un-correct," which features vocals from the legendary Merle Haggard on the album track. As a bonus cut, Gretchen is including a unique version of "Good Morning Heartache" from one of her favorite singers, Billie Holiday. *All Jacked Up* will be released in Canada and Australia on the same date.

"I was completely floored. I didn't even know what to say. . . . I certainly never expected female vocalist. . . . Everything just races through your mind, and you feel just really proud and really accepted and just really strong—even though at the same time you feel you're at the weakest you've ever been in your life. I love getting these awards, and I love being able to hold this certain amount of respect in my hand. But more so than the award, it just makes you feel so good to know that people accept you and people believe in you. It's been an amazing year for me."

—Gretchen Wilson backstage after receiving the ACM Top Female Vocalist award

GRETCHEN WILSON CHOKES BACK TEARS AS SHE ACCEPTS THE TOP FEMALE VOCALIST AWARD AT THE 40TH ANNUAL ACADEMY OF COUNTRY MUSIC AWARDS AT THE MANDALAY BAY RESORT AND CASINO IN LAS VEGAS, NEVADA ON MAY 17, 2005.